W9-ANX-466

Easter

By David F. Marx

Consultant
Katharine A. Kane, Reading Specialist
Former Language Arts Coordinator
San Diego County Office of Education

Children's Press®
A Division of Grolier Publishing
New York London Hong Kong Sydney
Danbury, Connecticut

Visit Children's Press® on the Internet at:
http://publishing.grolier.com

Designer: Herman Adler Design
Photo Researcher: Caroline Anderson

Library of Congress Cataloging-in-Publication Data

Marx, David F.
    Easter / by David F. Marx.
      p. cm. — (Rookie read-about holidays)
    Includes index.
    Summary: A simple introduction to Easter and some of the
ways it is celebrated.
    ISBN 0-516-22213-9 (lib. bdg.)   0-516-27175-X (pbk.)
    1. Easter—Juvenile literature. [1. Easter. 2. Holidays.]
I. Title. II. Series.
GT4935.M36   2001
394.2667—dc21
                               00-029453

Do you celebrate Easter?

This holiday always comes on a Sunday in March or April, just after the start of spring.

April 2001

Sunday	Monday	Tuesday	Wednesday	Thursday	Friday	Saturday
1	2	3	4	5	6	7
8	9	10	11	12	13	14
15	16	17	18	19	20	21
22	23	24	25	26	27	28
29	30					

People of the Christian religion celebrate Easter. They honor a man named Jesus Christ.

Christians believe that long ago Jesus came back to life after he died.

Easter is a celebration
of new life.

This holiday has a lot of
symbols (SIM-bulls). A
symbol is something that
has special meaning.

Eggs and bunnies are
Easter symbols. Easter
eggs can mean new life.

Easter bunnies can mean spring.

Many people enjoy
decorating Easter eggs.
First, an adult boils the
eggs so they get hard inside.

Then, the eggs are dyed, or colored, to make their white shells different colors.

Some people like to draw
on their eggs with crayons
or paintbrushes. Easter
eggs can be works of art!

Hunting for Easter eggs is a favorite holiday activity.

After adults hide the eggs, children have a lot of fun finding them.

Does your family bake Easter bread? Some people make it with Easter eggs baked inside.

On Easter, children hope
that the Easter Bunny will
bring them Easter baskets.

These baskets are often
filled with eggs, chocolate
bunnies, jellybeans, and
other treats.

Many Christians go to church on Easter morning.

Churches are decorated
with beautiful flowers,
such as white Easter lilies.

In some towns, there are Easter parades. Families walk through town dressed in their best new clothes.

The most famous Easter parade is in New York City. People show off their big, fancy Easter bonnets, or hats, in this parade.

After the parades, many families share special Easter meals.

They come together to wish each other, "Happy Easter! Happy spring!"

Words You Know

basket

bonnet

bread

eggs

Jesus Christ

lilies

parade

symbol

31

Index

About the Author

David F. Marx is an author and editor of children's books.
He resides in the Chicago area.

Photo Credits